D1566786

DIGGING UP THE PAST

THE PALACE OF KNOSSOS

BY EMILY ROSE OACHS

BELLWETHER MEDIA • MINNEAPOLIS, MN

TM

Are you ready to take it to the extreme? Torque books thrust you into the action-packed world of sports, vehicles, mystery, and adventure. These books may include dirt, smoke, fire, and chilling tales. **WARNING**: read at your own risk.

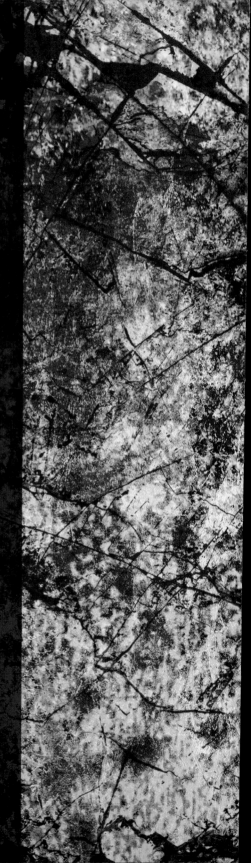

This edition first published in 2020 by Bellwether Media, Inc.

No part of this publication may be reproduced in whole or in part without written permission of the publisher. For information regarding permission, write to Bellwether Media, Inc., Attention: Permissions Department, 6012 Blue Circle Drive, Minnetonka, MN 55343.

Library of Congress Cataloging-in-Publication Data

Names: Oachs, Emily Rose, author.
Title: The Palace of Knossos / by Emily Rose Oachs.
Description: Minneapolis, MN : Bellwether Media, Inc., [2020] | Series:
    Torque : Digging Up the Past | Audience: Ages 7-12. | Audience:
Grades 3-7. | Includes bibliographical references and index.
Identifiers: LCCN 2018061016 (print) | LCCN 2019001667 (ebook) |
    ISBN 9781618916402 (ebook) | ISBN 9781644870686 (hardcover :
    alk. paper)
Subjects: LCSH: Palace of Knossos (Knossos)–Juvenile literature. |
    Excavations (Archaeology)–Greece–Crete–Juvenile literature. | Knossos
    (Extinct city)–Juvenile literature. | Crete
    (Greece)–Antiquities–Juvenile literature.
Classification: LCC DF221.C8 (ebook) | LCC DF221.C8 O33 2020 (print)
    | DDC 939/.18–dc23
LC record available at https://lccn.loc.gov/2018061016

Editor: Betsy Rathburn   Designer: Brittany McIntosh

Printed in the United States of America, North Mankato, MN.

TABLE OF CONTENTS

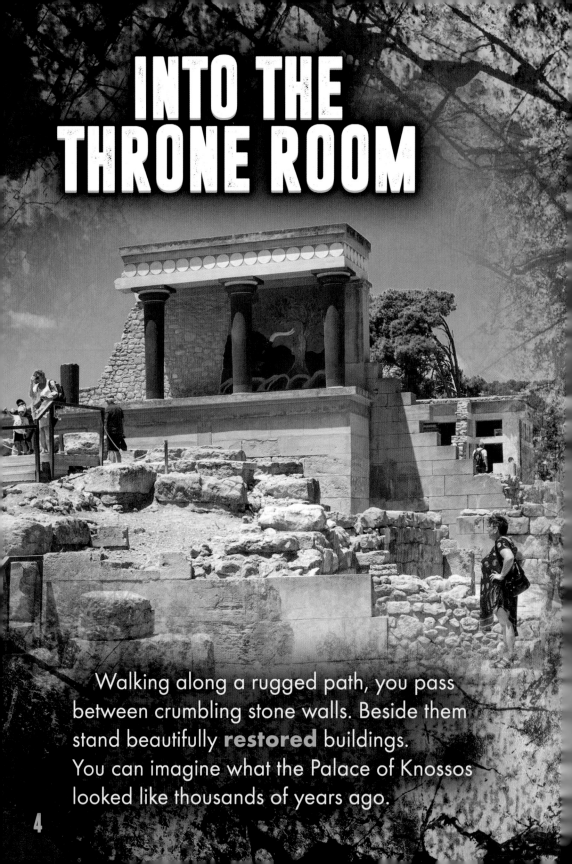

INTO THE THRONE ROOM

Walking along a rugged path, you pass between crumbling stone walls. Beside them stand beautifully **restored** buildings. You can imagine what the Palace of Knossos looked like thousands of years ago.

Next, you follow the path to the throne room. Bright **griffin** paintings color the walls. Against one wall stands a stone throne. A ruler may have once sat there!

griffin

throne room

5

WHAT IS THE PALACE OF KNOSSOS?

The Palace of Knossos is an **ancient** palace. It was built by the Minoan **civilization** about 4,000 years ago.

WHERE IS THE PALACE OF KNOSSOS?

N
W E
S

Greece

Palace of Knossos

THE OTHER PALACES

The Minoans built many palaces. Knossos was most important. Others were Phaistos, Malia, and Zakros.

The Minoans were most powerful between 1600 and 1400 BCE. They built several palaces on the Greek island of Crete. Knossos was the largest.

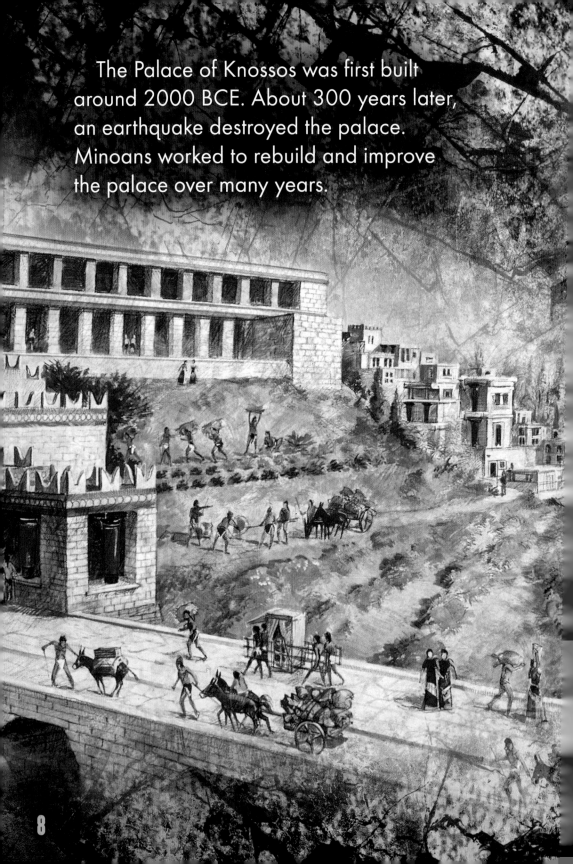

The Palace of Knossos was first built around 2000 BCE. About 300 years later, an earthquake destroyed the palace. Minoans worked to rebuild and improve the palace over many years.

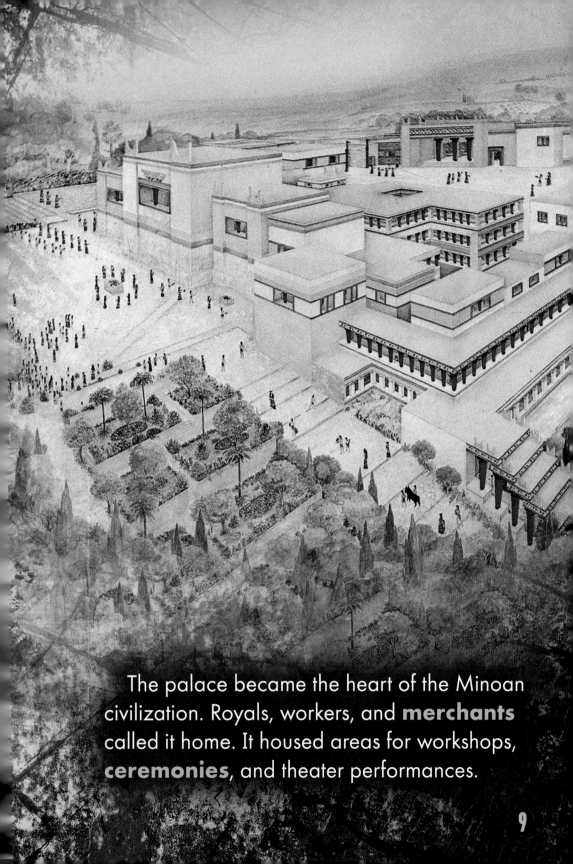

The palace became the heart of the Minoan civilization. Royals, workers, and **merchants** called it home. It housed areas for workshops, **ceremonies**, and theater performances.

Around 1450 BCE, an unknown disaster left the palace destroyed once again. A fire or **volcanic eruption** may have been to blame. In time, the Minoan civilization was wiped out. Some researchers believe it was **conquered** by **invaders**. The Palace of Knossos fell to ruin. Its remains now stand near Crete's capital, Heraklion.

PALACE OF KNOSSOS TIMELINE

about 3000 BCE:
Minoan civilization begins

about 1720 BCE:
An earthquake destroys the first Palace of Knossos and Minoans begin to rebuild

about 2000 BCE:
The first Palace of Knossos is built

about 1450 BCE:
The second Palace of Knossos is destroyed and abandoned

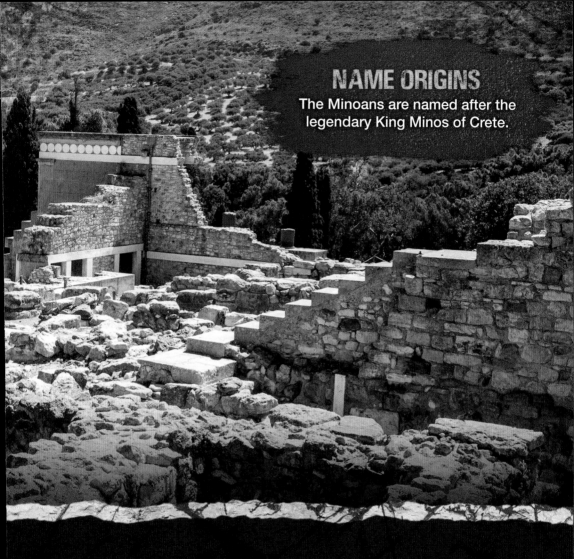

1878 CE:
Minos Kalokairinos finds part of the Palace of Knossos

1952 CE:
Michael Ventris learns how to translate Linear B writing from the palace

1900 CE:
Arthur Evans begins excavating

FINDING THE PALACE

Stories of the ancient palace lived on. The first person to find its **ruins** was Minos Kalokairinos. In 1878 CE, he discovered jars and other palace remains on his land.

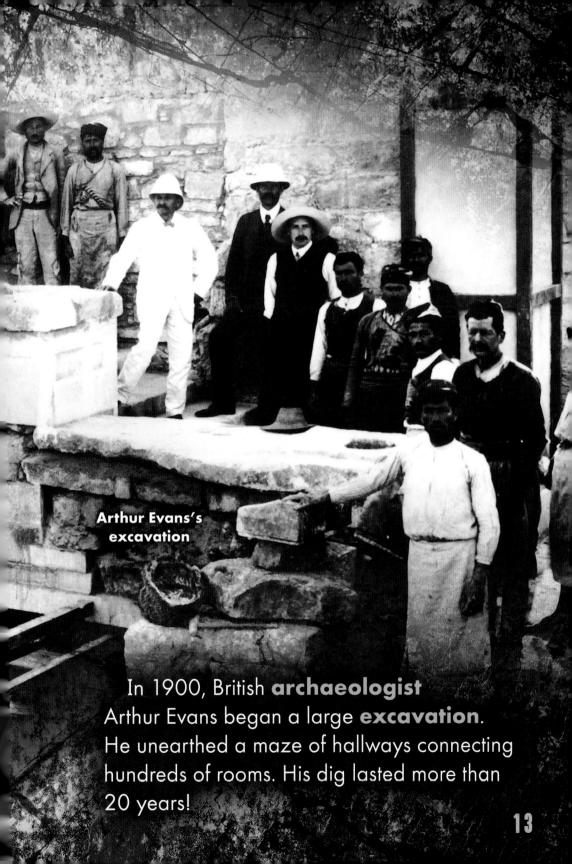

Arthur Evans's excavation

In 1900, British **archaeologist** Arthur Evans began a large **excavation**. He unearthed a maze of hallways connecting hundreds of rooms. His dig lasted more than 20 years!

13

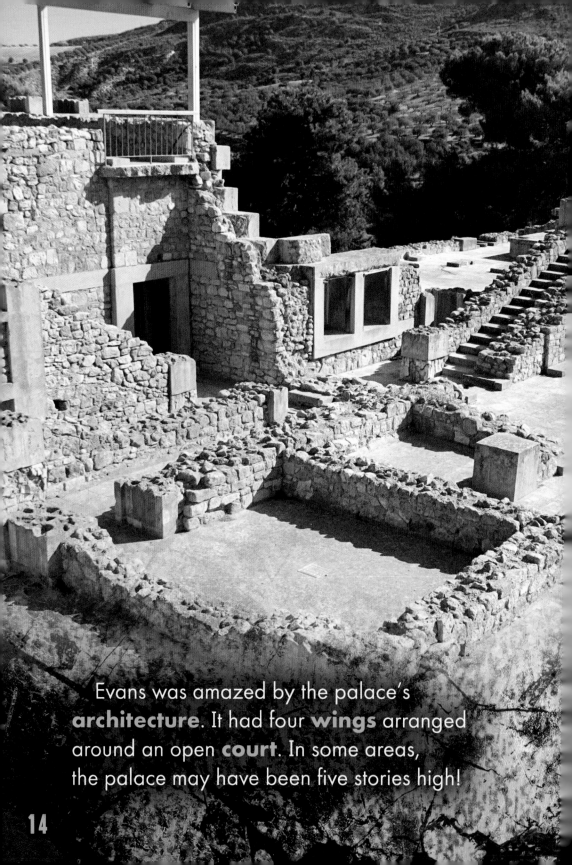

Evans was amazed by the palace's **architecture**. It had four **wings** arranged around an open **court**. In some areas, the palace may have been five stories high!

Inside, Evans found skilled artwork. There were many pieces of beautiful pottery. Colorful paintings called **frescoes** decorated the walls. Evans restored these to look as they might have 3,000 years before.

fresco

FRESCO PAINTINGS

The palace's frescoes show many different scenes. One shows a group of dolphins. Another shows a man jumping over a bull!

INDOOR PLUMBING

Minoans built pipes to bring water into Knossos. The palace may have even held the first-ever flushable toilet!

The palace also held thousands of clay **tablets** for keeping records. Three different styles of ancient writing were carved into them. In 1952, Michael Ventris became the first to **translate** the mysterious Linear B style.

Each find taught experts something new about the Minoans. The civilization had been long forgotten. But unearthing the palace brought its rediscovery!

MINOAN PALACE SIZES

Which Minoan palace was the biggest?

Knossos
215,000 square feet (20,000 square meters)

Phaistos
90,000 square feet (8,400 square meters)

Zakros
86,000 square feet (8,000 square meters)

Malia
80,700 square feet (7,500 square meters)

0   50   100   150   200   250

thousands square feet

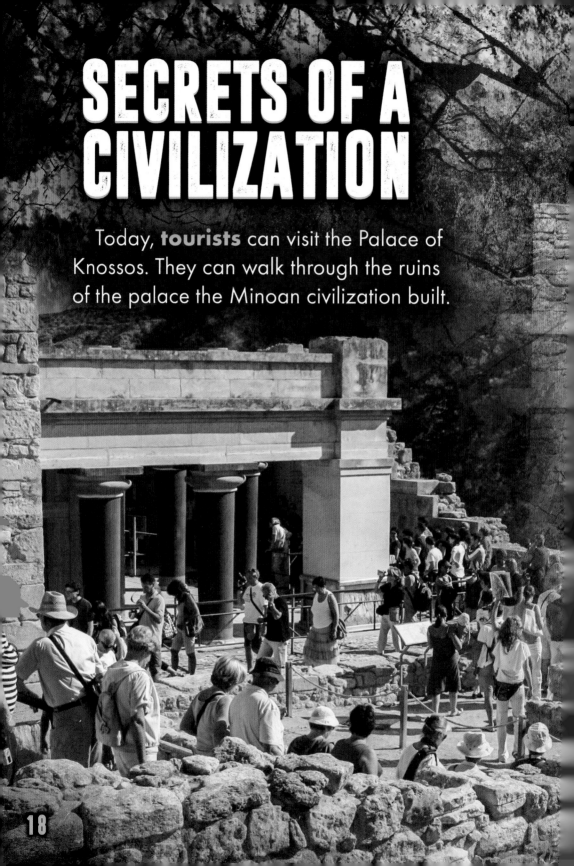

SECRETS OF A CIVILIZATION

Today, **tourists** can visit the Palace of Knossos. They can walk through the ruins of the palace the Minoan civilization built.

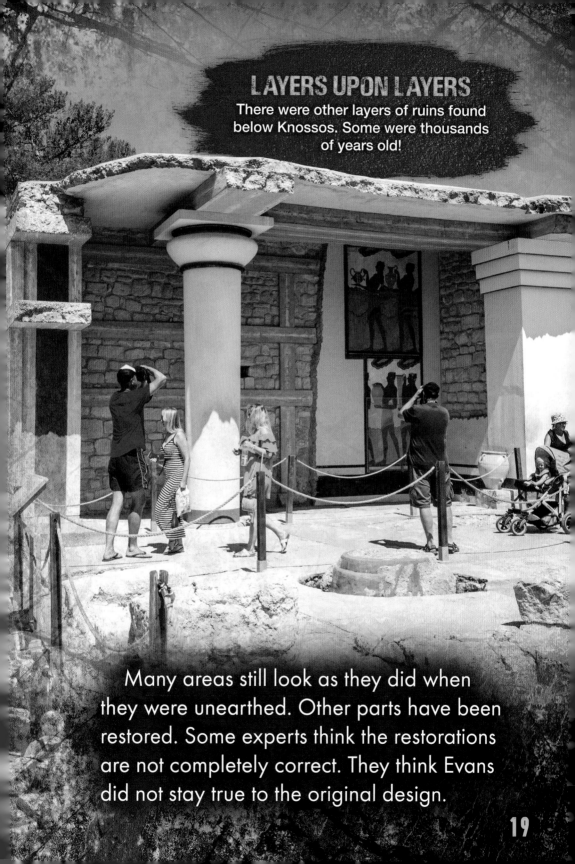

Many areas still look as they did when they were unearthed. Other parts have been restored. Some experts think the restorations are not completely correct. They think Evans did not stay true to the original design.

FORGOTTEN LANGUAGE

Discovery: Linear B writing style found at Knossos translated by Michael Ventris

Date of Discovery: 1952

Process:

1. Matched writing on Linear B tablets with writing found in other parts of Greece
2. Discovered that some of the Linear B writing was only on tablets found in Knossos
3. Recognized names of places on Crete on the Linear B tablets
4. Used translated place names to figure out other symbols

What It Means:

- Linear B tablets could now be read
- Lists of supplies and other records on the tablets showed how people lived
- Showed the Greek language has been used for much longer than previously thought

Visiting the palace is an important way to learn about the Minoans. It offers many clues about their civilization.

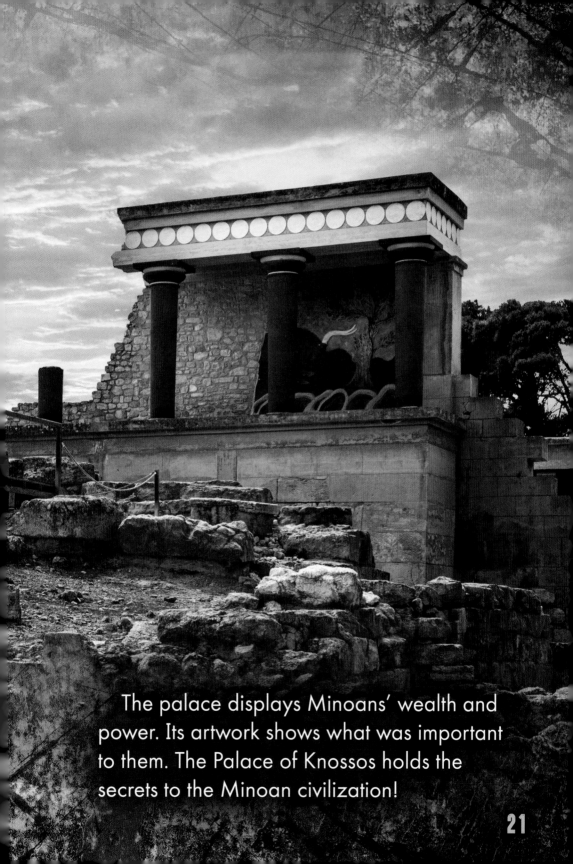

The palace displays Minoans' wealth and power. Its artwork shows what was important to them. The Palace of Knossos holds the secrets to the Minoan civilization!

GLOSSARY

ancient—very old

archaeologist—a scientist who studies the remains of past civilizations

architecture—the design of buildings and structures

ceremonies—events that mark important occasions

civilization—an advanced society

conquered—beaten or overthrown

court—an open space surrounded by buildings or walls

excavation—the act of digging up

frescoes—wall paintings

griffin—a mythical creature that is part lion and part eagle

invaders—people from one place who try to take over another place

merchants—people who buy and sell products to make money

restored—made fresh or rebuilt to look like an earlier form

ruins—the remains of a human-made structure

tablets—flat blocks used for writing

tourists—people who travel to visit another place

translate—to change one language into another language

volcanic eruption—an event in which hot lava comes out of a hole in the earth

wings—sections of buildings that lead out from a central area in different directions

TO LEARN MORE

AT THE LIBRARY

Faust, Daniel R. *Ancient Greece*. New York, N.Y.: Gareth Stevens Publishing, 2019.

Hoena, Blake. *Theseus and the Minotaur: A Graphic Retelling*. North Mankato, Minn.: Capstone Press, 2015.

Murray, Julie. *Greece*. Minneapolis, Minn.: Big Buddy Books, 2015.

ON THE WEB

FACTSURFER

Factsurfer.com gives you a safe, fun way to find more information.

1. Go to www.factsurfer.com.

2. Enter "Palace of Knossos" into the search box and click 🔍.

3. Select your book cover to see a list of related web sites.

INDEX

The images in this book are reproduced through the courtesy of: Georgios Tsichlis, front cover, pp. 16-17; IR Stone, p. 4; Dziewul, pp. 5, 10-11, 19; Duby Tal/ Albatross/ Alamy, p. 7; DeAgostini/ SuperStock, pp. 8, 12-13, 20; A. Burkatovski/ Fine Art Images/ SuperStock, p. 9; eFesenko, p. 14; Pecold, p. 15; dimakig, p. 18; Scorpp, pp. 20-21.